HANDS-ON HISTORY

PROJECTS ABOUT

Ancient Egypt

David C. King

Marshall Cavendish
Benchmark

New York

Acknowledgments

Many thanks to Sharon Flitterman-King for her creative work with crafts and recipes.

Benchmark Books
Marshall Cavendish
99 White Plains Road
Tarrytown, NY 10591-9001
www.marshallcavendish.us

Text Copyright © 2006 by Marshall Cavendish Corporation

Illustrations and map Copyright © 2006 by Marshall Cavendish Corporation

Library of Congress Cataloging-in-Publication Data
King, David C.
Projects about ancient Egypt / By David C. King.
p. cm.—(Hands-on history)
Summary: "Includes social studies projects taken from the ancient Egyptians"—Provided by publisher.
Includes bibliographical references and index.
     ISBN-13: 978-0-7614-2258-7
     ISBN-10: 0-7614-2258-7
1. Egypt—Civilization—To 332 B.C.—Juvenile literature. 2. Egypt—Civilization—To 332 B.C.—Study and teaching (Elementary)—Activity
     programs—Juvenile literature. I. Title. II. Series.
DT61.K448 2006
932—dc22
     2006002814

Title page: The Great Sphinx at Giza, Egypt.
Maps by XNR Productions
Illustrations by Rodica Prato
Photo research by Joan Meisel

Photo credits: *Art Resource*, NY: 10, Erich Lessing; 23, 42 *Scala; Corbis:* 1, Paul Hardy;
4, Aladin Abdel Naby/*Reuters*; 7, Nevada Wier; 8, Sandro Vannini; 15, Werner Forman; 20, 30,
Gianni Dagli Orti; 26, Roger Wood; 33, Royalty-Free; 35, *Bettmann*; 37

Printed in China

1 3 5 6 4 2

Contents

❧

1. Introduction 5

2. The River of Life 9

Paint

Small Brushes

Measuring Distance with Triangles

Midsummer Salad

3. The Good Life 21

Jeweled Collar

Wig

4. The Afterlife 31

Moving Blocks

Model Royal Coffin

Model Mummy

Glossary 45

Metric Conversion Chart 46

Find Out More 47

Index 48

Brilliant art adorns this bandaged mummy found near Cairo in 2005. Officials call the mummy the "most beautiful" found so far.

1

Introduction

Ancient Egypt—the words might make you think of the land of pharaohs and the Pyramids and the Great Sphinx. Or maybe you think of mysterious tombs containing the mummified remains of a pharoah who died more than thirty centuries ago.

In this book, you'll travel back in time to learn about one of the world's oldest civilizations, and one of the most remarkable. For three thousand years, beginning about 3100 BCE, Egypt created some of the building blocks on which later civilizations were built. The Egyptians made great advances in architecture, astronomy, art, and medicine. They developed **hieroglyphics**, one of the earliest forms of writing, and they discovered how to use a reed called **papyrus** to make the world's first paper.

This book will give you new ways of finding out about the fascinating world of ancient Egypt. You'll try your hand at writing hieroglyphics, even making your own ink and brush. You will also make the kind of wigs and jeweled collars that both men and women wore. You won't build a pyramid, but you can examine how huge blocks were moved. And, while you won't mummify anyone, you can make a model of a **sarcophagus**, or coffin, with a miniature mummy inside.

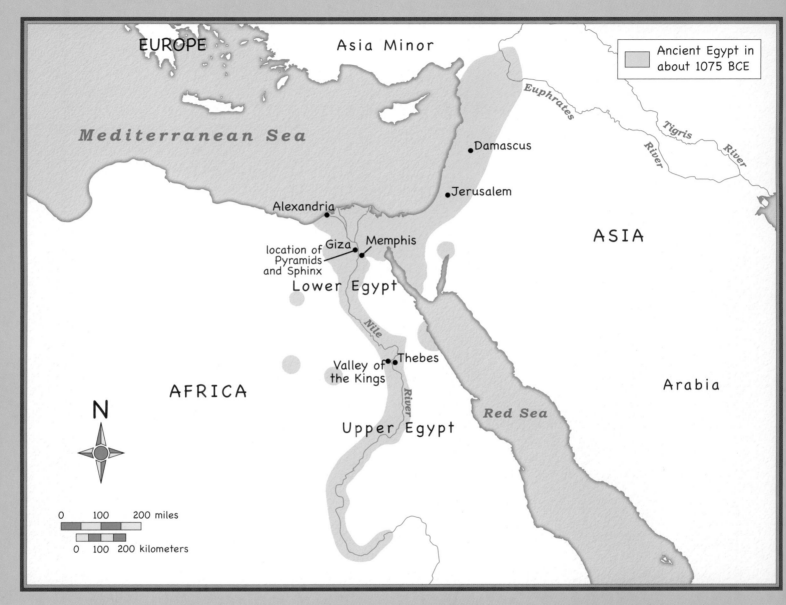

The land of the ancient Egyptians was mostly desert, which they called the "red land." Yet they called their entire country "Kemet," which meant "black land," referring to the rich, black soil deposited by the Nile flood.

Where the Egyptians Lived

Astronauts in earth-orbit can easily identify Egypt. From space it appears as a light brown patch in the northeast corner of Africa. This patch of desert covers the entire country except for a green strip running through it from south to north. The green is the valley of the Nile River, the longest river in the world. Although the fertile green area covers only 4 percent of Egypt's land, it made possible the great civilization of ancient Egypt.

The Nile overflows its banks in spring each year between July and October, following spring rains far to the south that feed the Nile. This flood brings rich soil from the hills and mountains far to the south. Over a course of more than 4,000 miles (6,400 kilometers), this fresh soil, called silt, enabled farmers to grow great amounts of grain and other foods. Because the farmland provided so much, many people were freed to build cities and towns, and to produce the material goods of a great civilization.

Wind and current patterns made the Nile River an excellent means of travel for the ancient Egyptians.

The Nile River during the flooding season. When the land was under water, farmers worked as laborers, perhaps building tombs or temples.

2
The River of Life

The fertile soil of the Nile River valley made Egypt's great civilization possible. That soil was used to grow wheat, barley, and a wide variety of other foods. It was used to grow flax for the linen used to make most of the clothing. It provided grazing land for cattle, and it produced the papyrus used to make furniture, boats, and sturdy sandals, as well as paper. The river also provided fish for food, water to drink, and a water highway for moving people and goods.

The flooding of the Nile each spring was crucial. If the flooding was too great, valuable land would be lost. And if the flooding didn't come, it could start a period of drought, during which crops withered and cattle died.

The importance of the Nile and its flooding made it essential that the Egyptians know how to measure accurately and how to keep good records. Every year's floods wiped out property markers, for example, so farmland often had to be **surveyed,** or measured, again. And because landowners paid part of their produce as taxes, accurate records had to be kept.

Important discoveries in math helped the Egyptians not only to measure land but also to take on tasks like building pyramids. And their writing system helped in business and government affairs, as well as in recording taxes and land-ownership.

Most of our knowledge of ancient Egypt comes from the stories, documents, and history recorded by ancient Egyptian scribes.

Hieroglyphics: Egyptian Writing

The year is 1751 BCE. As a young **scribe**, or writer, in the city of Thebes, you are still trying to master the Egyptian system of writing. You have worked hard through ten years of school, practicing on bits of pottery and flat stones. Now you can draw most of the picture symbols called hieroglyphs, so you are allowed to write on papyrus.

One reason the language has been hard to learn is that there are no vowels, no punctuation, and it can be read from left to right, or right to left, or even top to bottom. There is also the added difficulty of learning **hieratic script**—a kind of shorthand for hieroglyphics.

Although writing and chanting words all day has often been boring, you know the hard work is worth it. As a scribe, you will join an important profession. Scribes are paid well, live well, and are highly regarded.

Your first task today will be to make fresh paint and a brush. Fine lines can be made with a **stylus**, or pen.

Paint

You will need:

- one or two charcoal sticks or lumps (don't use briquettes)
- yellow, brown, and white chalk
- large paper plate or four small paper plates
- spoon
- two eggs
- water
- two small bowls
- four plastic cups
- stir stick or chopstick
- plastic wrap
- paper and pencil
- adult helper

1. Like the Egyptians, you'll make your paints from powders. Crush the charcoal and chalk pieces on a paper plate using the back of a spoon. Hold the spoon in one hand and push down with the other, using a grinding motion. Keep the four colors separate, and wipe off the spoon for each color.

2. Crack open the eggs carefully. Separate the eggs: the whites in one bowl, the yolks in another. (Ask an adult to help if this seems too tricky.) Save the yolks for a recipe or for scrambled eggs. Remember to wash your hands after handling raw eggs.

3. Spoon one powder into a paper cup. Add a little egg white and water. Use a stir stick or chopstick to mix the ingredients until you have a thick paint. The egg white acts as a binder, similar to that used by the Egyptians.

4. Repeat with the other three pigments. Cover each cup with plastic wrap.

5. Practice drawing the outline of some of the hieroglyphs shown on this page. Make each symbol large so that you can color it with a brush. Use a pencil as a stylus. You can also make one out of a strong reed, available at many florists. You will use your paints to color your hieroglyphs as soon as you make a brush.

desert, foreign country

"m" as in mouse

man

"w" as in wing

"k" as in kite

"j" as in joke

"t" as in top

"f" as in fish

"r" as in rug

"sh" as in shake

Small Brushes

You will need:

- a few strands of straw (available at florists and craft stores)
- scissors
- three or four thin dowels (⅛- or ¼-inch thick, 6 inches long), or a chopstick, or an unsharpened pencil
- three or four small rubber bands
- paper
- your paints—black, yellow, brown, white

1. Cut pieces of straw into three or four bundles—ten to twelve pieces about 3 inches long in each bundle.

2. Fit a bundle around a dowel, chopstick, or pencil. Twist a rubber band around the bundle as tightly as possible. Make sure the tips are even. Use scissors to trim the brush into a pointed tip.

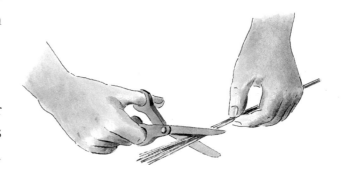

3. Dip the brush in water to moisten it a little, then dip it into one of the paints. Use small amounts of paint, and spread it evenly. Use another brush for the next color; or if you want to use the same brush, rinse it in water and move from a light color to a darker one. You're now ready to paint your hieroglyphs. The colors listed above were among those most commonly used in ancient Egypt.

Measuring Distance with Triangles

You are walking with your father along the banks of the Nile in the year 2221 BCE. The spring floods have ended, leaving rich, new soil that is so dark it is almost black. Ahead of you, you see two men stretching a rope between two stakes.

"Who are those men?" you ask. "Why are they on our property?"

"They are surveyors," your father explains. "We call them rope stretchers."

"Why?"

"Watch them. They're surveying, or measuring, the marsh where we harvest papyrus. They've placed a pole on the other side of the marsh. Do you see it? By measuring triangles on this side, they will know how far it is across the marsh to that pole. That way they won't get bogged down in the marsh."

"I still don't understand," you say.

"Just watch the rope stretchers."

Surveyors, or "rope stretchers," provided the careful measurements needed to build the temples and pyramids.

You will need:

- an open space outdoors to be the "marsh" (a parking lot or playground)
- three dowels or garden stakes, about 12 inches long. All three must be exactly the same length.
- four small pegs (scraps of wood or pencils)
- ball of string
- tape measure
- pencil
- paper
- helper

1. First, choose a tree or post on the far side of the "marsh." (You can place an object there if you have to.) You'll measure to this tree or other object. It will be point *X* on the diagram.

2. On your side of the marsh, lay the three dowels or sticks on the ground. Form them into a triangle, *ABC*. Position the triangle so that side *AB* points to *X*, as shown in the illustration.

3. Stick three pegs in the ground at the three points of the triangle. You can then remove the dowels.

4. Tie a string to the peg at point *A*. Stretch the string in the same direction as stick *AC* is pointing. (Don't let the peg at point *A* pull loose. Ask your helper to hold it.)

5. At point *F* along the string, set up your triangle of dowels again (*DEF* in illustration). This time, the line *EF* must line up with point *X*. If it doesn't, move the triangle right or left until you have a perfectly straight line, *EFX*.

6. Put your fourth peg in the ground at point *F*. Make sure the peg is firm. Tie the end of the string to this peg. (Don't cut the string; you can roll up the ball of string later.) Look at the large triangle on the diagram. The dotted lines form one large triangle *AXF*. It has the same shape as *ABC* and *DEF*. (These are called equilateral triangles because all sides are equal.)

7. How far is it across the marsh from *A* to *X*? It's the same distance as the string line from *A* to *F* because all sides of the triangle are the same length. Use the tape measure to find the distance from *A* to *F*. Have your helper hold one end.

Since you aren't measuring across a real marsh, you can check your results with the tape measure from *A* to *X*. Modern surveyors continue to work with this triangle method. You can also imagine how valuable this method would be in building the Great Pyramids, since the sides of the Pyramids are triangles.

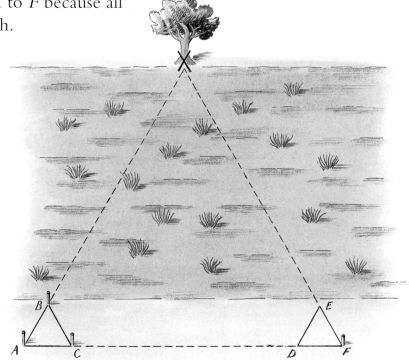

Midsummer Salad

On a hot summer day in December 1123 BCE, you are helping your mother prepare an evening meal of cold foods. She will serve it in the courtyard, where the water of the garden pool will cool the evening air. Windows in your house are placed high in the wall to reduce the noise and dust.

While your mother chops cucumbers into small pieces she has you prepare serving dishes with fresh dates, figs, and pomegranates. Cold sliced meat and barley bread will be served after the salad your mother is mixing. All of these foods have been produced on your family's farm. Your father is a government official and has hired workers and slaves to take care of the farm.

You will need:

- two large cucumbers
- 2 cups (1 pint) plain yogurt
- 2 teaspoons dill
- 4 teaspoons lemon juice
- salt and pepper to taste
- four or five mint leaves
- sharp knife
- cutting board
- large spoon
- mixing bowl and serving bowl
- plastic wrap
- adult helper

Makes 4 servings

1. With an adult's help, peel the cucumbers and dice them (cut into small pieces).

2. Place the diced cucumbers in a mixing bowl. Add the yogurt, dill, and lemon juice. Stir until the ingredients are thoroughly blended. Add a little salt and pepper to suit your taste.

3. Transfer the salad to a serving bowl. Top it with four or five fresh mint leaves (don't use dried mint).

4. Cover the salad with plastic wrap and chill it in the refrigerator for 10 to 15 minutes, or until you are ready to serve it.

This recipe is based on a modern Egyptian recipe called ancient-day salad. The yogurt is similar to an ancient Egyptian dressing made with goat cheese. Also, the lemon juice is a modern adaptation, since the Egyptians did not have lemons or other citrus fruits.

Wealthy families had gardens of palm or fig trees in the courtyard of their homes. There often were pools where brightly-colored fish from the Nile swam.

3

The Good Life

In most of the world's societies, 90 percent of the people were needed to produce enough food. This was even true in America until about 1800. Ancient Egypt was very different because the lush valley of the Nile could produce a great abundance of food. Over the centuries fewer and fewer people were needed for farming. This meant that more people could work in cities and towns.

Life was still hard for those at the bottom of the social ladder, including the poorest farmworkers and slaves. City workers, including bakers, carpenters, jewelry makers, and glassblowers, lived comfortable lives. They usually worked in shops with ten or more others, and many owned their own homes. Still higher up the ladder were wealthy merchants, government officials, priests, scribes, and landowners.

The wealthy lived in large homes made of sun-dried brick coated with plaster. Inside walls were painted with murals, or works of art. The kitchens and servants' quarters were in a separate building. The courtyard contained a pool, shade trees, and gardens. Scenes painted on tomb walls show that well-to-do families had frequent parties at which they enjoyed music, dance, games, and plenty of food and wine.

The pharaoh and his family were at the very top of Egyptian society.

Jeweled Collar

In the year 2717 BCE you are spending a day in the city of Abydos, a few miles from your family's villa. At a craft shop your mother is having a jeweled collar made.

"The collar for a man is very similar," the craftsman explains. "Of course, the size is likely to be different."

The craftsman shows your mother several samples for ideas and then looks at you. "And what about you?" he asks. "What color beads and stones would you like to have on your first neck collar? Perhaps you could draw a picture of it."

You will need:

- several sheets of newspaper
- pencil and scrap paper
- piece of felt, 16 or 17 inches square, light blue or tan (if necessary, substitute white cotton flannel)
- drawing compass
- tape measure and ruler
- scissors
- Velcro strips
- craft glue
- flat, plastic, colored disks or beads (available at craft stores)
- about thirty almond shells
- red, yellow, and blue poster paint
- small brush
- scraps of narrow ribbon and braiding

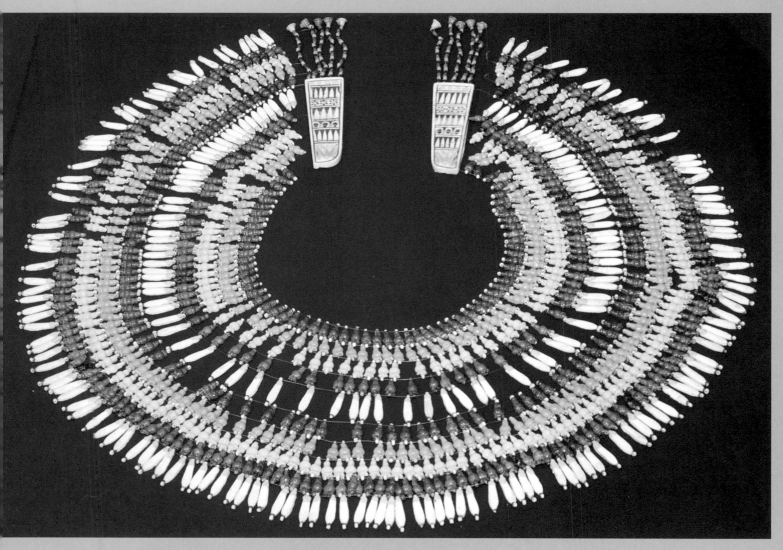

This beaded funeral collar was found in a pharaoh's tomb. Children in ancient Egypt wore collars, as well as earrings, bracelets, armlets and anklets.

1. Make a rough sketch on scrap paper of how you will place your decorations on the collar.

2. Spread a few sheets of newspaper on your work surface. Lay the fabric flat, and use the drawing compass to draw a circle on it about 16 inches across. (The radius—halfway across—will be 8 inches.) Cut out the circle of fabric.

3. Draw another circle five inches across in the center of your fabric. Cut out this smaller circle.

4. With a ruler, lightly draw a pencil line across the fabric through the center point. Make a second light line at right angles to the first. These lines will divide the cloth collar into four pie-shaped pieces. Cut out a piece that is a little smaller than one of those pie pieces, as shown in the drawing.

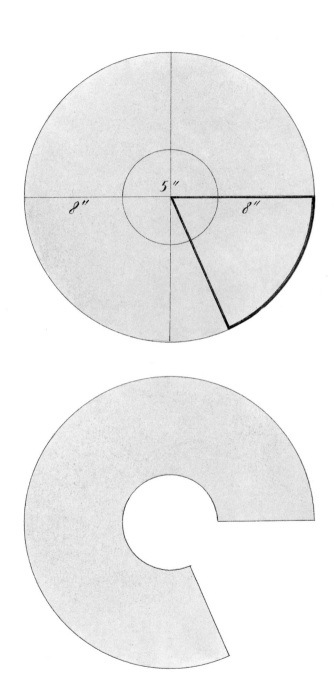

5. Place the collar around your neck to check the fit. There should be enough room for the ends to overlap by about an inch. If necessary, cut away a little more of the cloth. When the fit feels right, glue a Velcro strip on each end of the collar, one on the top of the fabric, the other on the underside. Set the collar aside for a few minutes.

6. Divide the almond shells into three equal piles. Paint the shells in each pile with a different color of poster paint. Set the shells aside to dry. Plan to apply a second coat if necessary.

7. Place the collar flat on your work surface, and glue the decorations on it following the arrangement in your sketch. The ancient Egyptians were fond of bright colors, so your finished neck collar will be in style.

Because of the glued items, the collar is more for display than for wearing. You might want to hang it on a wall of your room with thumbtacks or pushpins.

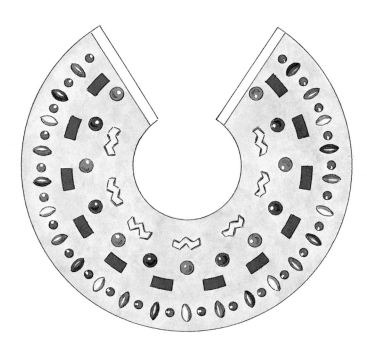

Ancient Egyptians wore wigs in fancy styles for special occasions. These were sometimes padded with vegetable fibers for more fullness.

Egyptian Wig

The year is 983 BCE. A woman is showing her daughter Ipwet how to use eye paint, face cream, and other cosmetics.

"The goddess called Hathor the Golden teaches us about beauty," Ipwet's mother explains. "Men as well as women spend time taking care of their appearance."

Ipwet is studying her mother's beautiful containers holding different liquids and powders. But she is also listening, and she says, "Maybe that's why my friend Nefertari has a name that means beautiful. She is so pretty."

Her mother laughs. "Wait until we finish with your cosmetics. You will be just as beautiful. Next we will make your wig. It will be even finer than your brother's new wig."

While many Egyptians had their heads shaved or closely cropped, those who cared about fashion wore wigs. Wigs for both men and women were made of human hair kept in place with beeswax. Children's hair was worn in a **sidelock** (pulled to one side), with part of the head shaved.

You will need:

- skein of black yarn
- piece of cardboard, about 8 inches by 11 inches
- strip of elastic fabric for a headband, 1 ½ to 2 inches wide, any color, long enough to go around your head with a little extra for overlap
- transparent tape
- scissors
- tape measure or ruler
- white glue or fabric glue
- piece of black felt, 10 to 12 inches square

1. Tape the start of the yarn to the cardboard. Wind the yarn around the cardboard from one side to the other, keeping the strands close together, as shown in the drawing. Cut the last strand, and tape it to the cardboard.

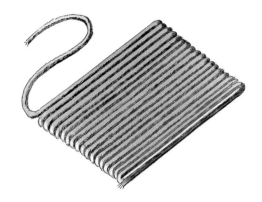

2. With scissors, cut through the yarn at one edge of the cardboard. Glue the folded end of each strand to the elastic headband. Begin 1 inch in from the left side of the elastic and glue strands for 5 inches; then glue for 5 inches from the right side, again with a 1-inch overlap. This will leave enough space in the middle for your face.

Note: Glue the strands only on one side of the elastic. This will be the inside of the headband, so the glued parts won't be seen.

3. Try on the headband. Pull it tight enough for a good fit, then glue the over-lapped ends. For a more permanent fit, sew the ends together, or have an adult help you with a sewing machine.

4. Cut the square of black felt in a circle to fit the top of your head. Place the circle on your head and carefully slide the headband over the circle and into position.

The third solid-gold coffin of Tutankhamen.

4

The Afterlife

The pharaoh was the most important person in ancient Egypt and the most powerful. He was believed to be a god as well as a man and was treated with great reverence. He ruled over what was then the world's largest empire, but he also had time for hunting, waging war, and with his queen, raising a family. He lived in a luxurious palace surrounded by his court and servants.

The ancient Egyptians believed in a life after death and that the deceased would need their bodies in that afterlife. This need led to the complicated process of making mummies to preserve the body, a process that only the wealthy could afford. The dead were also surrounded with things they might want or need, including furniture, clothing, and luxury items.

Many pharaohs had elaborate tombs built inside pyramids. Later rulers, from about 2100 BCE to 1000 BCE, had tombs built into the side of cliffs in the Valley of the Kings. Although all sorts of false tunnels and sliding blocks of granite were built into these resting places, grave robbers seem to have managed to loot them all—all, that is, except the tomb of Tutankhamen, which was discovered in 1922 CE.

Houses of Eternity

Some of ancient Egypt's most amazing achievements were in the engineering feats involved in building the Great Pyramids. Between 2700 BCE and 2200 BCE they built more than seventy of these "Houses of Eternity." With no machines or iron tools or wheels, they cut and moved gigantic rocks weighing up to seventy tons each. They needed two million or more of these blocks for a single pyramid.

The three most famous are the Pyramids at Giza. The largest, built by the pharaoh Khufu (or Cheops, in Greek), is called the Great Pyramid. It is sometimes said to be the greatest single building ever erected. The length of each side at the base is 755 ¾ feet (230.4 m) and the original height was 481 ⅔ feet (147 m). The 2,300,000 blocks required more than twenty years to put in place, with thousands of people working on it during the flooding season. Like most pyramids, the three at Giza were part of a compound that included a temple and several buildings to supply the pharaoh's needs in his next life.

The entrance to the Great Pyramid of Giza, also known as the Pyramid of King Khufu, or Cheops, as he was called in Greek.

Moving Blocks

The year is 2006 CE. You and your family are visiting the famous Pyramids at Giza. Your guide is explaining the Pyramid of King Khufu, completed about 2500 BCE.

"This is called the Great Pyramid," the guide says. "It is the largest of all, containing more than two million limestone blocks. The weight of the blocks ranges from just over two tons to fifteen tons each, and it took more than twenty years to put them all in place."

"How did they move all those blocks?" you ask.

"No one is entirely certain," she answers. "They may have used levers and rollers, but they had no pulleys—and of course, no machines."

"How much would the whole pyramid weigh?" your younger brother asks.

"You came to Egypt on a cruise ship? This pyramid would weigh as much as 250 of those ships."

This drawing shows workers, perhaps slaves, being forced to build the tombs and monuments of ancient Egypt. In fact, ordinary citizens helped to construct the Great Pyramids when they could not tend their fields during the flood season.

You will need:

- four or five large books, all about the same size
- string
- one rubber band
- ½ cup of sand
- eight or nine dowels, 8 to 10 inches long, or substitute round pencils

1. Choose a work surface that won't be damaged by the sand.

2. Place the books in a stack, and wrap string around them in two directions. This bundle will represent a three-ton limestone block that has to be moved to the pyramid.

3. Tie the rubber band to your block with a piece of string. You can now experiment with three different ways of moving a block:

A. Place the block on your work surface. Pull on the rubber band to drag it. Note how far the rubber band has been stretched.

B. Sprinkle sand on your work surface, and drag the block about the same distance. By reducing friction, the block will move more easily.

C. Now remove the sand, and place the rollers (dowels) on the work surface. Pull the block across them. The stretching of the rubber band should suggest how much the rollers have reduced the friction.

Model Royal Coffin

It is autumn, 1925 CE. Surrounded by Egyptian officials, archaeologist Howard Carter is opening the coffin of a young pharaoh named Tutankhamen. Carter had discovered the tomb three years earlier, the only tomb not completely ruined by grave robbers.

With great excitement Carter uncovered not one mummy-shaped coffin but three, one inside the other. The two outside coffins were made of wood covered with thin sheets of gold. The innermost coffin was made of solid gold.

Inside the gold coffin Carter saw the mummy of the young ruler. Tutankhamen's head and shoulders were covered by an extraordinary solid-gold mask, inlaid with semiprecious stones, like blue lapis lazuli. (The Egyptians had no precious stones, such as diamonds or rubies.)

Howard Carter, left, emerges from the tomb of King Tutankhamen holding a box of items collected for study. He wrote that the tomb contained "beautiful objects heaped upon one another."

You will need:

- a few sheets of newspaper
- two pieces of stiff cardboard, such as the back of a writing or drawing pad, about 8 inches by 10 inches
- one piece of thin, flexible cardboard, like a shirt board, at least 4 inches by 10 inches

- pencil
- ruler
- scissors
- white glue
- six to ten straight pins
- acrylic paint or poster paint
- small brush

1. Spread newspaper on your work surface.

2. On one sheet of the stiff cardboard, copy the drawing of the coffin base. Use the measurements provided in the illustration on page 39 to guide you. Use a ruler to make sure your measurements are exact. Cut out the base.

3. Now use the base as a template to make an exact copy of the base—place the base on the second piece of cardboard and trace around it. Cut out the second piece.

4. Glue the two base pieces together. Put this double-thick base under a stack of books until the glue is dry.

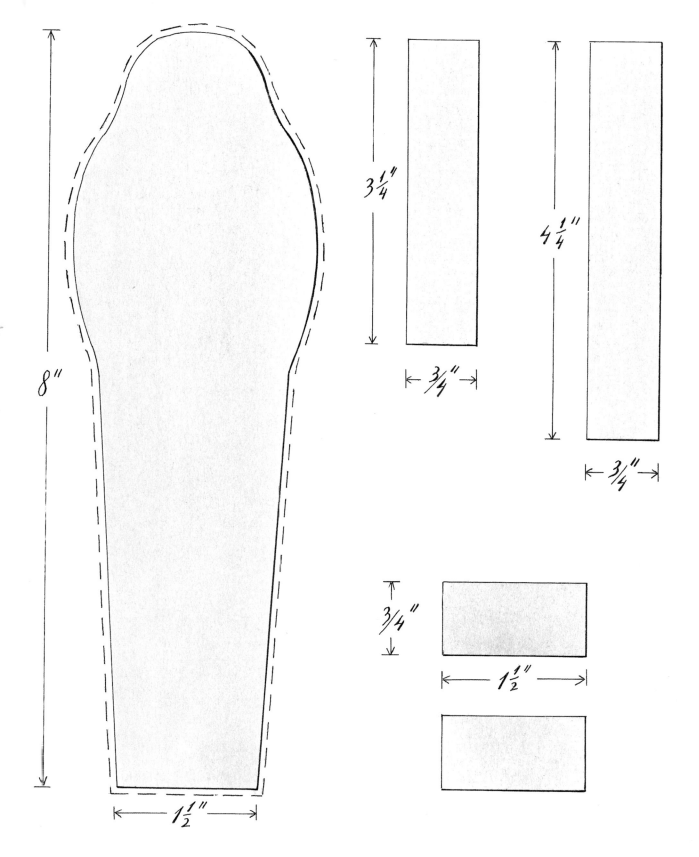

8"

3 1/4"

4 1/4"

3/4"

3/4"

1 1/2"

3/4"

1 1/2"

5. The lid has to be slightly larger than the base, as shown by the dotted lines in the drawing. Trace around your base piece with pencil; then draw a second line just outside the first, so your lid piece will be slightly larger than the base. You don't need a double layer for the lid.

6. Draw one side piece on the flexible cardboard, and cut it out. Use that piece as a template to cut out three more side pieces.

7. In the same way, make four foot pieces.

8. Each side piece should be 4 ¼ inches long. Put a thin ribbon of glue on the base and press the side piece against it. Hold the side in place until the glue takes over. Or you can hold it in place with a few straight pins. Put them in at a slight angle. Pull them out carefully when the glue is dry.

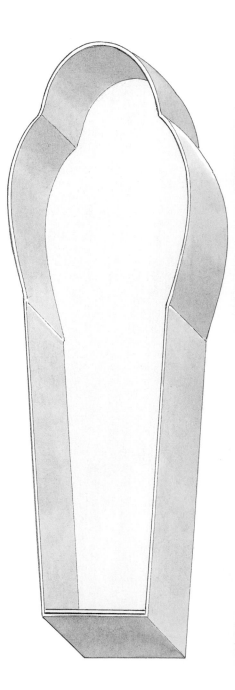

9. Repeat step 8 with the other side pieces and the two foot pieces.

10. When the glue has dried and the pins have been removed, place the lid on the base. Draw the face of the pharoah on the lid. You can add hieroglyphs to the lid as well, and to the sides of the lid.

The mummy of Ramses II, who ruled from 1279-1212 BCE. Although his tomb in the Valley of the Kings was destroyed by robbers, his mummy is one of the best-preserved ever discovered.

Model Mummy

In the year 1144 BCE **embalmers** are at work in the Beautiful House. They were preparing the body of a pharaoh for the afterlife. All of the organs except the heart have been removed. The brain is considered unimportant and is discarded. The other organs have been dried, wrapped in linen, and stored in special containers called **canopic** jars.

The body is packed in a chemical compound called **natron** for about forty days. This dries out the corpse and prevents further decay. The mummy is then wrapped in linen and carefully placed in its coffin. The pharaoh's **Ka**, or double, has not died, and the Ka can bring the mummy back to life.

You will need:

- a few sheets of newspaper
- self-hardening clay
- clean, white cotton rags (such as old sheets or T-shirts)
- ruler
- scissors
- white glue

1. Spread newspaper on your work surface. Work the self-hardening clay with your fingers to soften it.

2. Shape the clay into a human figure, with the arms folded on the chest and the legs together. Use a ruler to make sure your model mummy fits into the royal coffin you made. Follow directions on the clay package for letting it harden.

3. While the model hardens, cut narrow strips of white cotton to be the linen wrapping for the mummy. Make ten to twelve strips, each a few inches long.

4. Wrap the pieces of cotton around the figure, using a little glue to keep each strip in place.

5. Put the completed mummy in its coffin.

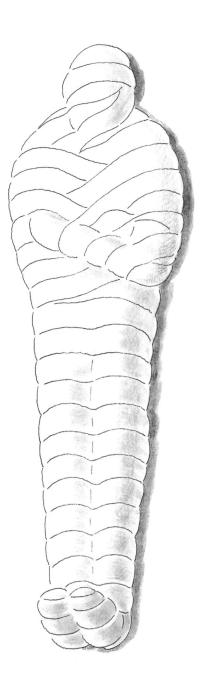

Glossary

canopic jars: Special containers for storing the organs of bodies being made into mummies.

embalmers: Experts in transforming a corpse into a mummy.

hieratic script: A shorthand version of hieroglyphics, used for ordinary documents such as business records.

hieroglyphics: The ancient Egyptian system for writing, using picture symbols called hieroglyphs.

Ka: The double of a deceased person who could bring a mummy back to life.

natron: A combination of chemical crystals used in making mummies.

papyrus: A reed growing in marshes along the Nile. The paper made from the reeds is also papyrus.

sarcophagus: A large coffin, often of stone, inside which the actual coffin is placed.

scribe: A writer.

sidelock: Long hair worn only on one side of the head, with the rest of the head shaved.

stylus: A pen, usually made from a strong reed, sharpened to a point.

surveyed: Measured, as in measuring land.

Metric Conversion Chart

You can use the chart below to convert from U.S. measurements to the metric system.

Weight
1 ounce = 28 grams
½ pound (8 ounces) = 227 grams
1 pound = .45 kilogram
2.2 pounds = 1 kilogram

Liquid volume
1 teaspoon = 5 milliliters
1 tablespoon = 15 milliliters
1 fluid ounce = 30 milliliters
1 cup = 240 milliliters (.24 liter)
1 pint = 480 milliliters (.48 liter)
1 quart = .95 liter

Length
¼ inch = .6 centimeter
½ inch = 1.25 centimeters
1 inch = 2.5 centimeters

Temperature
100°F = 40°C
110°F = 45°C
350°F = 180°C
375°F = 190°C
400°F = 200°C
425°F = 220°C
450°F = 235°C

About the Author

David C. King is an award-winning author who has written more than forty books for children and young adults, including *Projects About the Woodland Indians*, *Projects About the Spanish Southwest*, and *Projects About the Ancient Aztecs* in the Hands-On History series. He and his wife, Sharon, live in the Berkshires at the junction of New York, Massachusetts, and Connecticut.

Find Out More

Books

Hart, George. *Ancient Egypt*. New York: Alfred A. Knopf, Inc. and Dorling Kindersley, 1990.

Mellett, Peter. *Pyramids*. Milwaukee, WI: Gareth Stevens Publishing, 1998.

Tanaka, Shelley. *Secrets of the Mummies*. Madison, WI: Hyperion Press, 2001.

Woods, Geraldine. *Science in Ancient Egypt*. New York: Franklin Watts, 1988.

Wright, Rachel. *Egyptians*. New York: Franklin Watts, 1992.

Web Sites

Ancient Egypt: The British Museum
www.ancientegypt.co.uk/

Ancient Egypt Webquest
www.iwebquest.com/egypt/ancientegypt.htm

Daily Papyrus
www.virtual-egypt.com/

Mark Millmore's Ancient Egypt
www.eyelid.co.uk

Index

Page numbers in **boldface** are illustrations.

map, 6

afterlife, 31–32, 43
archaeology, 37, **37**
art, **4**, 21

building, 32, 34, **35**

children, 27
clothing, 9, 22–25, **23**, **26**, 31
cosmetics, 27

death. *See* mummies; tombs
desert, 7

education, 11

farming, 7, 9, 18, 21
food, 9, 18, 21
friction, 36

gardens, **20**
gods, 27, 31
gold and precious stones, **30**, 37

hair, 27. *See also* wigs
hieroglyphs, 11, **12**
homes, 9, 18, **20**, 21, 31–32.
    See also tombs

land
    flooding, 7, **8**, 9, 14, 32
location, **6**, 7
    ownership, 9

mathematics, 9
measurement, 9, 14, **15**
metric conversion chart, 46
mummies, **4**, 31, 37, **42**, 43, **44**

names
    of country, 6
    of people, 27
Nile River, **7**, 7–9, **8**

papyrus, 5, 9, 14
parties, 21
pharaohs, 21, **30**, 31, 32, **42**, 43
projects
    cooking, 18–19
    hieroglyphics, 11–13
    jeweled collar, 22–25, **23**
    measuring, 16–17
    moving blocks, 36
    mummy, 43–44
    sarcophagus, 38–41, **41**
    wig, 27–29
pyramids, **6**, 31, 32–34, **33**

record keeping, 9, **10**

slavery, 18, **35**
socioeconomic classes, **20**, 21
sphinxes, 5, **6**, **35**
surveyors, 9, 14

tombs, 21, **30**, 31, **35**, 37–41.
    See also pyramids
travel, **7**, 9
Tutankhamen, **30**, 31, 37

Valley of the Kings, 31, 42

wigs, **26**, 27–29
writing, 5, 9–13, **10**